Touching

by Helen Frost

Consulting Editor: Gail Saunders-Smith, Ph.D.

Consultant: Eric H. Chudler, Ph.D.
Research Associate Professor
Department of Anesthesiology
University of Washington, Seattle

Pebble Books

an imprint of Capstone Press
Mankato, Minnesota

Pebble Books are published by Capstone Press
1710 Roe Crest Drive, North Mankato, Minnesota 56003.
www.capstonepub.com

Library of Congress Cataloging-in-Publication Data
Frost, Helen, 1949-
     Touching/by Helen Frost.
     p. cm.—(The senses)
     Includes bibliographical references and index.
     Summary: Uses simple text and photographs to explain how the sense of
touch works.
     ISBN-13: 978-0-7368-0386-1 (hardcover)
     ISBN-10: 0-7368-0386-6 (hardcover)
     ISBN-13: 978-0-7368-4872-5 (softcover pbk.)
     ISBN-10: 0-7368-4872-X (softcover pbk.)
     1. Touch—Juvenile literature. [1. Touch. 2. Senses and sensation.] I. Title.
II. Series: Frost, Helen, 1949- The senses.
QP451.F93 2000
612.8'8—dc21   99-14307
                                                                                              CIP

Note to Parents and Teachers

The Senses series supports national science standards for units
related to behavorial science. This book describes and illustrates
the sense of touch. The photographs support early readers in
understanding the text. The repetition of words and phrases helps
early readers learn new words. This book also introduces early
readers to subject-specific vocabulary words, which are defined in
the Words to Know section. Early readers may need assistance to
read some words and to use the Table of Contents, Words to Know,
Read More, Internet Sites, and Index/Word List sections of
the book.

Printed in the United States of America in North Mankato, Minnesota.
042013   007305R

Table of Contents

Touching. 5

What You Feel 9

How Touch Helps You 21

Words to Know 22

Read More 23

Internet Sites. 23

Index/Word List. 24

Touching is one of your five senses. You use your skin to touch.

Sensors in your skin receive signals when you touch things. Nerves carry the signals from your skin to your brain. Your brain understands what your skin feels.

Some sensors tell you if things are hot or cold. Fire is hot. Snow is cold.

Some sensors tell you if things are light or heavy. A feather is light. A rock is heavy.

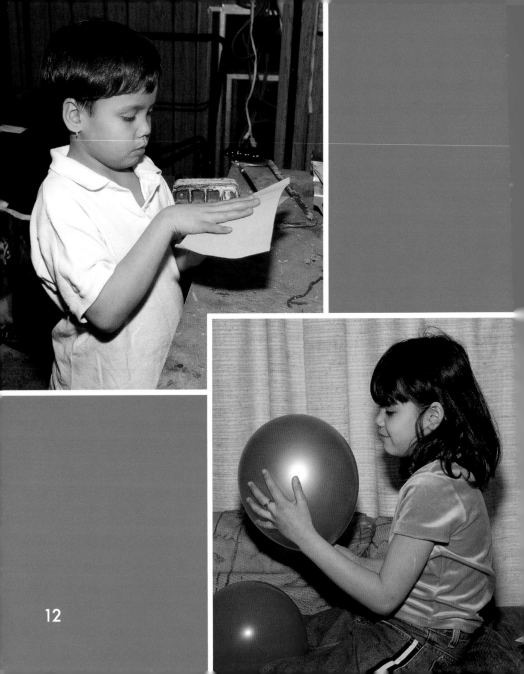

Some sensors tell
you if things are
rough or smooth.
Sandpaper is rough.
A balloon is smooth.

Some sensors tell you
if things move or stay
still. A puppy moves.
A desk stays still.

Some things you touch feel good. Soft fur feels good.

Some things you touch cause pain. Touching a cactus causes pain.

Pain warns you of danger. Your sense of touch helps you stay safe.

Words to Know

brain—the body part inside your head that controls your body; your brain understands what your skin touches.

nerve—a bundle of thin fibers that sends signals between your brain and other parts of your body; nerves in your skin are important for your sense of touch.

pain—a feeling of hurt

sense—a way of knowing about things around you; touching is one of your five senses; hearing, seeing, smelling, and tasting are your other senses.

sensor—a cell that detects things and sends signals to your brain

signal—a message; your skin sends signals to your brain.

skin—the outer tissue on your body; sensors in your skin detect things you touch.

Read More

Ballard, Carol. *How Do We Feel and Touch?* How Our Bodies Work. Austin, Texas: Raintree Steck-Vaughn, 1998.

Hurwitz, Sue. *Touch.* Library of the Five Senses and the Sixth Sense. New York: PowerKids Press, 1997.

Pluckrose, Henry. *Touching and Feeling.* Senses. Austin, Texas: Raintree Steck-Vaughn, 1998.

Internet Sites

FactHound offers a safe, fun way to find Internet sites related to this book. All of the sites on FactHound have been researched by our staff.

Here's all you do:

Visit *www.facthound.com*

Type in this code: 9780736803861

Index/Word List

balloon, 13
brain, 7
cactus, 19
cold, 9
danger, 21
desk, 15
feather, 11
feel, 17
fire, 9
fur, 17
heavy, 11

hot, 9
light, 11
move, 15
nerves, 7
pain, 19, 21
puppy, 15
rock, 11
rough, 13
safe, 21
sandpaper, 13
sense, 5, 21

sensors, 7, 9,
   11, 13, 15
signals, 7
skin, 5, 7
smooth, 13
snow, 9
soft, 17
still, 15
touch, 5, 7,
   17, 19, 21

Word Count: 142
Early-Intervention Level: 14

Editorial Credits
Mari C. Schuh, editor; Timothy Halldin, cover designer; Kimberly Danger,
   photo researcher

Photo Credits
David F. Clobes, 10 (top and bottom), 12 (top and botom), 16, 18, 20
Dianne Meyer, cover
Index Stock Imagery/Roger Holden, 14 (bottom)
Photo Network/Myrleen F. Cate, 1; David Wheelock, 8 (top)
Shaffer Photography/James L. Shaffer, 6
Uniphoto, 8 (bottom), 14 (top)
Visuals Unlimited/Peter Holden, 4

24